Dogs to the Rescue!

by Jilly Hunt

CW00552617

Say the sounds.

/yoo/	-ue *as in rescue*
/long oo/	-ue *as in glue*
/yoor/	-ure *as in pure*
/chu/	-ture *as in picture*

Blend the sounds to read the words.

statue	pictures	clues
secure	rescue	<u>s</u>ure

Dogs can help us. We can train them.

This person cannot hear. The dog helps him to cross the road.

Sam cannot see. The dog helps him on the stairs.

Dogs help at the shops.
Sue is sure it is her turn. She trusts her dog.

Dogs can help if you feel sad.

Farmers train dogs for jobs on the farm.

Turn the ducks to the left!

A sheepdog can collect the sheep.
The sheep will be secure in the pen.

This dog helps with the cows.
The cows go to the farmland to feed.

This is a rescue dog. A trekker
is missing!

lost trekker

The dog looks for the lost man.
It sniffs for clues.

Dogs swim to the rescue.

This dog has a jacket on to help it float.

Dogs can jump in from rescue boats.
This dog is a good swimmer.

This statue is to thank a helpful dog.

Look at the pictures. They are all good dogs that helped.

Hudson

Bowser

Finn

Boo

Talk together

1. How can dogs help on a farm?

2. How do dogs look for lost people?

3. Look at the dogs below. What people can they help?